Fill My Heart with Love

Fill My Heart with Love

30 Days of Prayer with Methodist Women

PAUL W. CHILCOTE

CASCADE *Books* · Eugene, Oregon

FILL MY HEART WITH LOVE
30 Days of Prayer with Methodist Women

Cascade Books
An Imprint of Wipf and Stock Publishers
199 W. 8th Ave., Suite 3
Eugene, OR 97401

www.wipfandstock.com

PAPERBACK ISBN: 978-1-6667-0814-1
HARDCOVER ISBN: 978-1-6667-0815-8
EBOOK ISBN: 978-1-6667-0816-5

Cataloguing-in-Publication data:

Names: Chilcote, Paul Wesley, 1954–, author.

Title: Fill my heart with love : 30 days of prayer with Methodist women / Paul W. Chilcote.

Description: Eugene, OR : Cascade Books, 2021 | Includes bibliographical references and indexes.

Identifiers: ISBN 978-1-6667-0814-1 (paperback) | ISBN 978-1-6667-0815-8 (hardcover) | ISBN 978-1-6667-0816-5 (ebook)

Subjects: LCSH: Methodist women—History—18th century. | Methodist women—History—19th century. | Spirituality—Methodist Church—History—18th century. | Spirituality—Methodist Church—History—19th century.

Classification: BX8345.7 .C45 2021 (paperback) | BX8345.7 .C45 (ebook)

12/15/21

For my granddaughter,
Elsie Rose Glass,
who was born with
a heart full of love

Contents

An Invitation

I WANT TO INVITE you into a spiritual adventure. In this book you have an opportunity to learn from women by praying prayers derived from their spiritual writings and by singing songs of faith composed by women. You will be amazed by the insights they offer about God, authentic living, and your place in the journey. I love to prepare devotional books. The preparation of such a book becomes my own practice of prayer. Each phase of the production reveals something new to me about God, myself, and the community joined together in prayer. Writing this book has been my own act of prayer. I also know that people need this kind of resource in order to grow in their faith and in their relationship with God. For many people—maybe even most—prayer is not an easy thing. John Wesley once advised an early Methodist who was struggling in her life of prayer to pray the prayers of others until the Spirit guided her into her own way—until she discovered her own voice. That was good advice. So preparing a resource to help engage you in meaningful ways with the living God by introducing you to phenomenal spiritual guides simply delights me.

But why have I—a man—collected these prayers and songs of women and provided them to you here? Would it not be better for me to leave this kind of work to women? I admit that these are good and legitimate questions deserving a straightforward answer. Essentially, through my own use of this rich collection of prayers and hymns, these women have taught me how to be a better person of prayer. I have placed myself at their feet. Without them, I truly do not know what my own life of prayer would be like. Certainly I would be the poorer for their absence. So I want to honor that influence and celebrate those discoveries about God, life, and love. I offer this book to you so that you too can celebrate the spirituality of these women. I would love for you to have the opportunity to immerse yourself in this world, because I believe these prayers and hymns offer a vision of enduring value to all God's children today.

I have published a number of devotional resources, but this book aligns with two others in particular. In *Praying in the Wesleyan Spirit*, I "translated" John Wesley's so-called "standard sermons" into the forms of prayer in order to make them more accessible to the contemporary reader. Using the same approach, I "translated" a host of devotional and theological materials from John Wesley's *Christian Library* in a book entitled *Praying in the Spirit of Christ*. In this third book, then, I "translate" the writings of Methodist women into the forms of prayer. Some of these texts were designed originally as prayers, but even these I have modernized to connect more fully with a contemporary reader. The fact that women authored all the material I have translated into prayers and the lyrical texts of the hymns I have chosen makes this volume unique.

In the minimal editorial work I have done on the prayers, I have been very intentional in my use of inclusive language. Given the fact that most of the sources are drawn from the eighteenth and nineteenth centuries, this has presented some challenges. With regard to the hymns, I made the decision to retain the language as presented in the *United Methodist Hymnal*, since careful editors attended to this issue when the hymnal was in preparation during the 1980s. I always want to be inclusive. My hope is that, in those selections where I made the decision to retain non-inclusive language, this does not create a barrier to anyone who seeks to meet God in these readings. My primary intention throughout has been to let the women speak in their own unique voices and to capture their spirit in winsome contemporary forms of prayer.

I pray that you will engage this rich treasury of Christian devotion by reading it, pondering it, singing it, and then, hopefully, by putting it into practice. The Spirit breathed life into the original women who authored these texts, and the Spirit longs to breathe new life into you as you open yourself to the spiritual insight and wisdom of these mentors in the faith. Permit the Spirit to shape you through these rich resources. They have shaped the lives of countless generations of men, women, and children who have met God in prayer and song.

Paul W. Chilcote
The Feast Day of St. Brigid of Kildare

Introduction

O how precious are your ways to my soul,
suited to my weakness, worthy of a God!
I live moment by moment upon your smiles
and dwell under the shadow of your wings.
I desire nothing but to please you,
to grow in inward conformity to your will
and sink deeper into humble love,
to let the light of what your grace has bestowed
shine on all around,
and to live and die proclaiming
God is love. Amen.

THIS PRAYER OF HESTER Ann Rogers introduced me to the world of women's spirituality. Hetty, as she was known, was an early Methodist woman in England and a close friend of John and Charles Wesley. This prayer has traveled with me on every step of my journey. It has shaped my life in more ways, most likely, than I can even imagine. The way this young woman prayed exemplifies, to me, what it means to pray with authenticity.

In the studies on early Methodist women's spirituality I have conducted over the years, several particular characteristics continue to stand out. You can sense these themes in their devotional lives—in the prayers they produced and the reflective practices in which they engaged.

First, they reflect a spirituality of pathos in which they explore the mystery in life. At a time when most mothers could expect only about half their children to survive beyond five years of age, Mary Entwisle poured out her heart to God in prayers like this one:

> What can I possibly return to you, O God,
>   for all your bountiful blessings to me?
>   I have so much for which to be grateful.
> You are such a kind preserver who has cared for me
>   beyond my wildest dreams.
> You supported me through the hour of my trial.
> You answered my prayers
>   and brought me safely and easily through.
>   May I trust you at all times!
> You made me the living mother of a living child!

Second, they exhibit a spirituality of beauty in which they marvel at the majestic in life. Mary Hanson illustrates this spirit in her observations about nature and the wonders of creation:

> How delightful is the contemplation of your works, O God!
>   My enraptured eye runs over your handiwork in
> creation
>   with a curiosity and interest that never leave me.
> The passing clouds, the opening flowers,
>   the sweet river, whose constant changes
>   give a variety to the scenes.
> How frequently these stimulate my imagination,
>   and often, how inexpressible is my gratitude
>   for receiving so many outward blessings
>   from your hands, O God.

Third, they proclaim a spirituality of love in which they celebrate the miracle in life. One of the most noteworthy women of early Methodism, Mary Fletcher, preached and prayed much about love. You could even say it was the hallmark of her ministry—a salient theme transparent in this prayer:

> O blessed fountain of love,

> fill my heart more with your divine principle!
> Sink me lower in the depths of humility,
> and let me sit at the feet of Jesus and learn of him.
> May his love fill my heart, as the Scripture expresses it,
> "the love of God, shed abroad in your hearts
> by the Holy Ghost, given unto you."
> If I get my heart full of your love, O God,
> I know that this is the oil
> by which the lamp of faith
> will be ever kept burning.

Most of the women featured here come from the early period of the Methodist movement in eighteenth-century England. Many of their names will be new to you. But the women featured here include some of the early women preachers, like Sarah Crosby and Mary Fletcher. Many of these women functioned as pioneers with positions of leadership in Wesley's Methodist Societies. Others simply left behind the record of their spiritual lives in journals and correspondences, a practice strongly encouraged by the Wesleys. The singular exception to these early Methodist women is Georgia Harkness, a modern American theologian of great renown, whose life and witness I simply could not leave out. I provide a brief biographical introduction to all the women in this volume—both the authors of the prayers and the hymn writers—at their first appearance in the text. I hope this helps "put a face on them" and helps you appreciate their vision of the Christian life more fully.

I have drawn most of the material here from two of my earlier publications, *Her Own Story: Autobiographical Portraits of Early Methodist Women* and *Early Methodist Spirituality: Selected Women's Writings*. In addition to these sources, one selection comes from the collected works of Susanna Wesley, and a number of prayers are based on excerpts from Georgia Harkness's autobiographical work, *Grace Abounding*. All the hymns included in this volume are from the *United Methodist Hymnal* (UMH). They feature eighteen women hymn writers and translators. You will note that two lyricists, in particular, stand out in terms of their presence here, with six selections each. Fanny Crosby, without question the most prolific woman hymn writer of all time, was a Methodist, so she has a special place here among her Methodist sisters. Catherine Winkworth, a British Unitarian, is one of the most famous translators of ancient, classic hymns. Through the use of her unique literary gifts, she made each text her own. But this constellation of women hymn writers represents a wide spectrum of Christian traditions.

The structure of this devotional book follows that of the hymnal directly. There is a theological structure, therefore, to this book, reflecting the Methodist lyrical heritage. The devotional readings move from a Trinitarian platform—celebrating the nature and work of the Father, Son, and Holy Spirit—through the way of salvation—examining the various aspects of life in God—to the community of faith and its work in the world—reminding the community of its reason for being and the goal toward which we all move. I have divided these broad themes into five parts: "The Glory of the Triune God," "The Grace of Jesus Christ," "The Power of the Holy Spirit," "Holiness of Heart and Life," and "The Community of Faith."

These readings, along with the hymn selections that accompany them and the Scripture texts that provide their orientation, represent a rich treasury of spiritual insight. The questions, concerns, and commitments of the women writers span a broad spectrum. But their engagement with the realities of life, their amazement at the majestic nature of creation, and their quest to both experience and express the depth of God's love shine through their prayers and their hymns. My hope is that you will make their spiritual wisdom your own as you read, ponder, and put these devotional readings into practice. As you pray through the language of these women, open your heart to the God of love.

Suggestions for Using
This Devotional Material

MY SUGGESTIONS FOR USING these devotional readings are very simple. Those who engage in spiritual practices regularly know the importance of space, time, and even posture. Find or create a space in which to reflect and pray. Hopefully, it is a quiet place where you can be as still and undisturbed as possible. Meeting with God in this space at the same time each day can really be helpful to the process of settling your spirit. Many people find the early morning the best time for prayer and reflection. Others prefer the evening. But you need to determine what works best for you with regard to your circumstances and daily rhythms.

Even posture can be helpful in terms of focus. In my own experience, my general rule in this regard is comfort. Relax. Settle in. This is not a test. Be gracious with yourself and open to the Spirit. Simply prepare to spend some quality time with the God you love—and who loves you deeply—as if you are spending time with a cherished friend.

DAILY PATTERN
Centering Bible Text
The Prayer
The Hymn
Silent Reflections:
Journaling/Discussion
Blessing

I do invite you to read this book following a Daily Pattern. It is very simple, consisting of six elements. I have provided a brief *passage from the Bible* to provide focus for your time of prayer and meditation. The selected text for each devotion locates the topic of each prayer and hymn within the larger world of the biblical witness. Your journey through these devotional materials begins, therefore, by immersing yourself in the fertile soil of God's Word. Pray before you begin and ask God to open your heart and life to the presence of Christ through the Spirit. Permit God to speak to you through the word.

Following some moments of silence, *pray the prayer*. Do not rush. Read slowly and deliberately. You may want to read through the entirety of the prayer or you may find it helpful to pause at natural breaks or as the Spirit guides you. Ask yourself what aspects of the prayer touch you or relate to you most directly.

Again, following a moment of silence *"sing" through the hymn*. If the hymn is familiar to you, you may actually want to sing it out loud. Before you begin your time of devotion, you may want to locate a recording of the hymn selection so you can hear it performed or sing along. Let the memories flow. Hymns touch us deeply. If the hymn is new to you, attend to God's presence and purpose in the words. One of the great saints of the early church said that to sing is to pray twice. Hopefully, the inclusion of these hymn texts will enable the Spirit to touch your life in a different way than the prayers themselves.

After having prayed and read or sung the hymn, embrace just a few moments of *silent reflection* on the whole of your experience. Let the words that linger revolve around naturally in your mind. Be attentive to how this makes you feel. Let God's love flow around you, over you, and through you.

I provide a question at the conclusion of each devotion and space in the book for personal *journaling*. This question can also be used for the purposes of *discussion* if you are using this resource in a small group. On the basis of reports from those who have used *Praying in the Wesleyan Spirit* and *Praying in the Spirit of Christ*, I highly recommend that you find a way to share this experience with others. Journeying through this material in a group—prayer groups, covenant discipleship groups, Bible studies, class meetings—multiplies insight and enhances the benefit to your spirit. Whether you use the questions for journaling or discussion (or both), they are meant to prompt reflection; you need not be slavish in following them. Feel free to mark this book up with your comments and reflections, as the Spirit leads.

Conclude each day's time of reflection with a prayer of gratitude to God or with this *Blessing* based on Romans 15:13:

> *God of hope, fill me with all joy and peace as I trust in you,*
> *so that I may overflow with hope by the power of the Holy Spirit.*
> *Amen.*

If you are a pastor, feel free to use any of these materials in Sunday or midweek worship experiences where you can provide others an opportunity to sink their buckets into this deep well of spiritual insight from these women mentors of the past. Be attentive to the Spirit's voice as you read these texts. Most assuredly, you can find wonderful material here for sermons and Sunday school classes! You may also find the various indexes I have supplied at the end of the book to be helpful in using it.

Open yourself to the leading of the Spirit. In whatever way you choose to use this book, approach the experience prayerfully. Ask God to speak to you through the insights of these great women of faith. You may even want to begin each reading with the simple prayer: "Lord, you speak to me through your word, the hymns of the church, and words from the great cloud of witnesses. Open my heart to hear your voice through these words today." Once you have pondered their words, the Scripture text, and the women's hymns that "sing the theme" for each devotion, seek to live out God's vision in your daily life. God, most certainly, will accompany you in this journey.

PART 1

The Glory of the Triune God

An Introductory Comment

The prayers and hymns of women in the first segment of this volume celebrate the three persons of the Trinity, the God we know as Father, Son, and Holy Spirit—the One who creates, redeems, and sustains all life. Their words reflect a strong credal sense of the God revealed in the sacred Scriptures of the Judeo-Christian heritage. The women believe that this one true God is worthy of praise and thanksgiving. They seek to abide in this God—the One who provides. Their writings depict a God who fills us all with hope and love.

1

One True God

Scripture:

Hear, O Israel: The Lord is our God, the Lord alone. You shall love the Lord your God with all your heart, and with all your soul, and with all your might. Keep these words that I am commanding you today in your heart.

—Deuteronomy 6:4–6

Prayer:

Blessed Father, Loving Jesus, Holy Spirit!
    You are the one true God, and I will be yours every moment.
        I give myself again to you. Give yourself again to me!
Beloved Father!
    I revere your majesty and sink before you.
        You are a holy God. I submit my all to you.
        I wonder at your glory every moment!
Blessed Jesus!
    You are my constant friend and companion.
        You are always with me.

You show me the Father and I am lost in beholding his glory.
   You take me out and bring me in.
You are my constant pattern and continual help.
Holy Spirit!
   You are my comforter.
      I feel from you a constant burning love.
      My heart is set on fire by your blessed influence.
   I pray by your power.
      I am brought to Jesus through you
         and through Jesus I am brought to the Father.
In you, the one true God, I am swallowed up in what I call glory.
Glory be to the Father, glory be to the Son,
   and glory be to the Holy Spirit! Amen

—Ann Cutler, *Account*

Ann Cutler (1759–1794), affectionately known as "Praying Nanny," was born in Lancashire and died in the Methodist stronghold of Macclesfield. She was famous among all the Methodists of her day for her life of prayer. Despite opposition, she prayed frequently in public and was in constant demand to pray with people who found themselves in difficulties of any kind. The details of her life are known primarily from the *Account* of her life published by the great Methodist revivalist William Bramwell, which consisted almost entirely of her journal.

Hymn:

We believe in one true God,
Father, Son, and Holy Ghost,
ever present help in need,
praised by all the heavenly host;
by whose mighty power alone
all is made and wrought and done.

We believe in Jesus Christ,

Son of God and Mary's Son,
who descended from his throne
and for us salvation won;
by whose cross and death are we
rescued from sin's misery.

We confess the Holy Ghost,
who from both fore'er proceeds;
who upholds and comforts us
in all trials, fears, and needs.
Blest and Holy Trinity,
praise forever be to thee!

—UMH 85 (trans. Catherine Winkworth)

Catherine Winkworth (1827–1878), one of the most famous translators of classical hymns, particularly those of the Middle Ages and German culture, campaigned vigorously for women's education in Bristol towards the end of her life. Her translations remain some of the best-known of all hymns in the English language, many of which are included in this book.

Engage:

How have I sought to express my love to this Triune God today?

Reflections:

2

Praise and Thanksgiving

Scripture:

> Let them thank the LORD for his steadfast love,
>   for his wonderful works to humankind.
> For he satisfies the thirsty,
>   and the hungry he fills with good things.
>
> —Psalm 100:8–9

Prayer:

O Lord God, Maker of heaven and earth!
  You made all things by your word and for your glory!
Father of all, I acknowledge you as the author of my being,
  the preserver of my life, and the giver of every good
    and perfect gift.
  I submit myself to you as my sovereign Lord and loving parent.
    I have sinned and am not even worthy to be called your child.
    But I bring myself to you—a creature of your own making.
  I humbly offer myself to you so that you can continue your
  work in my life.

Create me anew after your own image,
so that I might be your faithful servant as long as I live.
O blessed Jesus, plead my cause with your Father.
I am ready to profess myself your disciple
upon your own terms and to follow you.
I give up myself to your teaching and instruction.
O give me understanding that I may know the truth as it is
in you.
I ascribe all the honor for my redemption and restoration
to your self-giving sacrifice and eternal intercession.
I put my trust in you alone.
O life-giving Spirit, I owe everything to you.
I will be attentive to your impulses whenever I sense them,
because you lead me away from brokenness and death
into the way of life.
I give myself to you—O Father, Son, and Holy Spirit—with my
whole heart.
Fill me with praise and thanksgiving.
Give me a glad and generous heart. Amen.

—Joanna Cook, *Spiritual Experience*

Joanna Cook (1732–1784) exerted a significant influence upon early Methodism. In 1751, she wrote a prayer that she used for the purpose of her covenant renewal with God. It became popular throughout the movement after appearing in her *Spiritual Experience*. Deeply rooted in the Puritan heritage of English Christianity, the practice of an annual renewal of one's commitment to God became a central aspect of early Methodist spirituality. It marks the need for recurrent acts of dedication to God and the way of Christ throughout one's life.

Hymn:

To God be the glory, great things he hath done!
So loved he the world that he gave us his Son,

who yielded his life an atonement for sin,
and opened the lifegate that all may go in.
Refrain:
Praise the Lord, praise the Lord,
let the earth hear his voice!
Praise the Lord, praise the Lord,
let the people rejoice!
O come to the Father thru Jesus the Son,
and give him the glory, great things he hath done!

O perfect redemption, the purchase of blood,
to every believer the promise of God;
the vilest offender who truly believes,
that moment from Jesus a pardon receives.
(*Refrain*)

—UMH 98:1–2 (Fanny Crosby)

Frances "Fanny" Crosby (1820–1915), the blind "queen of the gospel song," was one of the most prolific hymn writers in history, with over eight thousand compositions. A woman of warm evangelical faith, she was converted under Methodists in New York City and thereafter engaged in outreach to the poor. Crosby's hymns have been translated into over one hundred languages.

Engage:

Describe how you were attentive to a spiritual impulse recently and what happened.

Reflections:

3

Abiding in Christ

Scripture:

Abide in me as I abide in you. Just as the branch cannot bear fruit by itself unless it abides in the vine, neither can you unless you abide in me. I am the vine, you are the branches. Those who abide in me and I in them bear much fruit, because apart from me you can do nothing.

—John 15:4–5

Prayer:

Glory, honor, and eternal praise to you, O Christ, for ever and ever!
    Your own arm has brought salvation to my feeble, helpless soul.
        I am now wholly yours!
I love you, O God, with all my heart, and soul, and strength.
        I am nothing and Jesus is my all.
            The enemy often suggests,
                "You will soon lose the blessing;
                You cannot stand long."
            But my heart answers,

"I will hang upon and trust my God
as long as I have any being,
and I know Christ will supply me with power!"
I am so thankful for all you have done for me, O Christ.

Enlarge my faith's capacity,
Wider and yet wider still
Then with all that is in thee
My soul forever fill.

Abide in me as I abide in you, O Lord.
As the branch cannot bear fruit unless it abides in the vine,
neither can I unless I abide in you.
Your intimacy with me is such a blessing;
my soul draws near to you and gives thanks for you each day.
Amen.

—Hester Ann Rogers, *Experience*

Hester Ann Rogers (1756–1794) married James Rogers, one of Wesley's preachers, and shared his itinerant life in both Ireland and England. Hetty was famous among the Methodists of her day for her eminent holiness, zeal, and Christian influence. Her fame was due in large measure to the publication of extracts from her journal, first appearing in 1796 as *The Experience of Mrs. Hester Ann Rogers*. This book reveals a profoundly interior spirituality, revolving around the joy she experienced through abiding in Christ.

Hymn:

Now thank we all our God,
with heart and hands and voices,
who wondrous things has done,
in whom this world rejoices;
who from our mothers' arms
has blessed us on our way
with countless gifts of love,
and still is ours today.

O may this bounteous God
through all our life be near us,
with ever joyful hearts
and blessed peace to cheer us;
and keep us still in grace,
and guide us when perplexed;
and free us from all ills,
in this world and the next.

—UMH 102:1–2 (trans. Catherine Winkworth)

Engage:

How has abiding in God sustained you through difficult times?

Reflections:

4

God's Provision

Scripture:

> I lift up my eyes to the hills—
>   from where will my help come?
> My help comes from the LORD,
>   who made heaven and earth.
> The LORD will keep
>   your going out and your coming in
>   from this time on and forevermore.

—Psalm 121:1-2, 8

Prayer:

O God, my help,
I am so often consumed with worry and feel overwhelmed.
I want to feel my heart more disentangled from outward things
    so I can enjoy a more meaningful communion with you.
Right now, I especially need an unshaken confidence in you.
I want to be able to cast my every care upon you.
Lord, be with me in the fast approaching hour.

Bring me safely through the birth of my beloved child.
Spare me to my friends and my dear family,
    if it is your blessed will.
What can I possibly return to you, O God,
    for all your bountiful blessings to me?
    I have so much for which to be grateful.
You have cared for me beyond my wildest dreams.
    You supported me through the hour of my trial.
    You answered my prayers and brought me safely through.
You made me the living mother of a living child!
    No one could have taken care of my every need as you did.
    You carried me through.
You kept my going out and my coming in,
    and I know you will forevermore.
I will never forget your care, your provision, your peace.
    I trust in you. Amen.

               —Mary Entwisle, Manuscript Diary

Mary Entwisle (c. 1770–1804), the wife of a Methodist itinerant preacher, left behind a fascinating but brief thirty-two-page diary. It portrays the fragile and tragic nature of life for women in her time. It includes her honest reflections on the perils of childbirth, the perennial threat of disease, and the inner strength found in faith. Covering the brief six-year period between 1793 to 1798, this manuscript account provides a realistic, true-to-life portrait of discipleship in the midst of tragedy and pervasive uncertainty.

Hymn:

Be not dismayed whate'er betide,
God will take care of you;
beneath his wings of love abide,
God will take care of you.
Refrain:
God will take care of you,

through every day, o'er all the way;
he will take care of you,
God will take care of you.

All you may need he will provide,
God will take care of you;
nothing you ask will be denied,
God will take care of you.
(*Refrain*)

—UMH 130:1, 3 (Civilla Martin)

Civilla Martin (1866–1948), a native of Nova Scotia and a village school teacher, composed comforting gospel songs with her husband, a Baptist itinerant evangelist. Her two most famous songs, this one and "Why Should I Feel Discouraged" ("His Eye Is on the Sparrow"), are featured in this volume.

Engage:

How has God's provision brought great joy to you recently?

Reflections:

5

Praise of God

Scripture:

Praise the LORD!
Praise, O servants of the LORD;
    praise the name of the LORD.
Blessed be the name of the LORD
    from this time on and forevermore.
From the rising of the sun to its setting
    the name of the LORD is to be praised.
The LORD is high above all nations,
    and his glory above the heavens.

—Psalm 113:1–4

Prayer:

You are worthy of praise, O Lord! Most high God!
Accept my gratitude for your past and present blessings,
    and let your bountiful goodness
        lead me to walk humbly with you always.
You have demonstrated your love to me through every step

I have taken in obedience to you, my heavenly Guide.
    You have directed me on a path to the mansion of peace.
Whatever you require of me, enable me to do by your power,
    and may I be attentive to the Spirit at all times,
        so that I might have access to your
        immediate help in all things.
Blessed be your name, O Lord of hosts.
    Your love is eternal and the splendor of your riches
        in grace increase
    while all earthly gems and treasures grow dim with age.
I pray that my delight in you will increase day by day;
    that I might pursue the way of life and the path of peace,
        might be swallowed up into your immensity
        and lost in your love, O God, my only friend.
You are worthy of praise, O Lord! most high God!
    Your praise will always be on my lips.
        Blessed be the name of the LORD. Amen.

—Dorothy Ripley, *Account*

Dorothy Ripley (1769–1831), a native of Yorkshire, was strongly influenced by both Methodist and Quaker preachers. In 1801, she felt a special call to work among the American slaves and actually interviewed President Thomas Jefferson and addressed Congress on the topic of social reform and the abolition of slavery in particular. She made the Atlantic crossing some eight or nine times, expanding her work in America to include prison reform and Native American advocacy. This prayer is adapted from one of her two autobiographical works.

Hymn:

Praise to the Lord,
the Almighty, the King of creation.
O my soul, praise him,
for he is thy health and salvation!

All ye who hear,
now to his temple draw near;
join me in glad adoration!

Praise to the Lord,
who doth prosper thy work and defend thee;
surely his goodness
and mercy here daily attend thee.
Ponder anew
what the Almighty can do,
who with his love doth befriend thee.

Praise to the Lord!
O let all that is in me adore him!
All that hath life and breath,
come now with praises before him!
Let the amen sound from his people again;
gladly forever adore him.

—UMH 139:1, 3, 5 (trans. Catherine Winkworth)

Engage:

Describe the most immediate reason you have to praise God today.

Reflections:

PART 2

The Grace of Jesus Christ

An Introductory Commentary

Jesus figures prominently in the spirituality of the women included in this devotional resource. They proclaim the light of his glory and exalt his name in prayer and song. The prayers and hymns here follow the progression of Jesus' life from the mystery of the Incarnation through the Cross to the triumph of the Resurrection. This review of his life and ministry of grace puts a song of gladness in the heart.

6

The Name of Jesus

Scripture:

> At the name of Jesus
>   every knee should bend,
>   in heaven and on earth and under the earth,
> and every tongue should confess
>   that Jesus Christ is Lord,
>   to the glory of God the Father.
>
> —Philippians 2:10–11

Prayer:

All glory to you, Lord Jesus!
   Oh! Your unbounded love to my soul!
Good Shepherd, your promises are all precious.
Word of God, my peace flows as a river
   while you teach me the lessons of your grace, of faith, and holiness.
Living Water, my soul is thirsty for all the mind that was in you.

> Lord, take my heart and let it be
>   Forever closed to all but thee:

Seal thou my breast, and let me wear
That pledge of love for ever there.

Sun of Righteousness, you shine on my soul without a cloud
between.
Blessed Redeemer, what a delight I feel in all your blessed ways!
Son of God, your service is my reward.
Immanuel, I long to live to you in your presence
as I have never done before.
Lamb of God, my love abounds to you for your mercy and grace.
Giver of Life, my soul is like a watered garden.
Risen Lord, my heaven here consists in glorifying you.
Glorious Savior, praised be your name.
Master and Guide, keep me at your feet
and I shall praise you more and more. Amen.

—Isabella Wilson, *Diary*

Isabella Wilson (1765–1807) was an important instrument of revival in the north of England under John Wesley's direction. The little we know about her life must be gleaned from her diary, excerpts of which were published by John Pipe following her death. Her diary is a truly remarkable document, reflecting her total confidence in the presence and power of God. Gratitude and thanksgiving are the consistent keynotes of her daily entries. All the selections in this volume are taken from this diary.

Hymn:

At the name of Jesus every knee shall bow,
every tongue confess him King of glory now;
'tis the Father's pleasure we should call him Lord,
who from the beginning was the mighty Word.

In your hearts enthrone him; there let him subdue
all that is not holy, all that is not true.

Crown him as your captain in temptations hour;
let his will enfold you in its light and power.

—UMH 168:1, 4 (Catherine Noel)

Catherine Noel (1817–1877), a devout Anglican, wrote her first hymn as a teenager. The hymn featured here was the signature text of a collection entitled *The Name of Jesus, and other Verses for the Sick and Lonely*. As someone who struggled with health issues throughout her life, most of her compositions were intended for private mediation and comfort in the midst of sickness.

Engage:

Which "name of Jesus" has been most meaningful to you over the years, and why?

Reflections:

7

Jesus Comes

Scripture:

> Lift up your heads, O gates!
>   and be lifted up, O ancient doors!
>   that the King of glory may come in.
> Who is this King of glory?
>   The Lord of hosts,
>   he is the King of glory.

—Psalm 24:9–10

Prayer:

I lift up my heart to you, O wondrous Child
  and know that you are watching over me
    even in this very moment as I pray.
  Because you have come, I no longer ask,
    "What do you want from me?"
  Rather, my heart cries out,
    "I believe and love, and abide in you forever!"
      Jesus, come, and fill me with love divine.

I lift up my head to you, O wondrous Child.
and know that you are a compassionate King
who rules this world with grace and truth.
My spirit is free from hurry and confusion,
for you work in a composed and quiet mind.
I abide in the full expectation of your love
and trust you to do in me far more than I imagine.
Jesus, come, and fill me with love divine.
I lift up my life to you, O wondrous Child.
and ask you to take all my will and affections
that they may be ever focused on you above all else.
Your promises are wide and deep;
your love is like a broad river—a stream of living water.
Nothing secures the crown upon your head
as my readiness to believe that you save us to the uttermost.
Jesus, come, and fill me with love divine. Amen.

—Mary Fletcher, *Life*

Mary Fletcher (1739–1815), whose maiden name—Bosanquet—reveals her Huguenot stock, stands without a rival in the annals of early Methodism. In addition to her roles as preacher, advisor, counselor, small group leader, minister's wife, and patron, she was a prolific writer. While her *Life*—extracts from her journals and letters—was certainly the most well-known of her writings, her various tracts and circular letters made their way into every corner of British Methodism. This extract, taken from her *Life*, demonstrates her profound witness to God's love.

Hymn:

Lift up your heads, ye mighty gates;
behold, the King of glory waits;
the King of kings is drawing near;
the Savior of the world is here!

Fling wide the portals of your heart;
make it a temple, set apart
from earthly use for heaven's employ,
adorned with prayer and love and joy.

Redeemer, come, with us abide;
our hearts to thee we open wide;
let us thy inner presence feel;
thy grace and love in us reveal.

—UMH 213:1–3 (trans. Catherine Winkworth)

Engage:

How is Jesus born anew into your heart day by day?

Reflections:

8

The Mystery of Incarnation

Scripture:

In that region there were shepherds living in the fields, keeping watch over their flock by night. Then an angel of the Lord stood before them, and the glory of the Lord shone around them, and they were terrified. But the angel said to them, "Do not be afraid; for see—I am bringing you good news of great joy for all the people: to you is born this day in the city of David a Savior, who is the Messiah, the Lord. Glory to God in the highest heaven, and on earth peace among those whom he favors!"

—Luke 2:8–11, 14

Prayer:

O lovely Jesus!
   Blessed Jesus!
      Adorable Jesus!
Glory! Glory! Glory! Glory!
   To God in the highest!
      On earth peace, good will towards all!

Incarnate Lord, you came down and lived among us
in order to raise us up to the abundant life of love.
You want every single person to live,
and you have given yourself
that whoever believes in you shall never perish.
O precious Jesus!
My beloved is mine and I am his!
He is the fairest of ten thousand and altogether lovely.
Incarnate Lord, you came down and lived among us
in order to raise us up to the abundant life of love.
O what glory do I see!
And all is for me!
My soul burns with love to Jesus.
I see fountains upon fountains,
rivers of grace and mercy,
oceans of love in which I will swim to all eternity.
Incarnate Lord, you came down and lived among us
in order to raise us up to the abundant life of love.
Amen.

—Mary Langston, *Journal*

Mary Langston (1749–1769) was awakened spiritually under the preaching of Methodist itinerants during her teen years. She demonstrated the importance of the means of grace in her spiritual development and was diligent in her participation in prayer, the study of Scripture, fellowship with other Christians, and the Sacrament of Holy Communion. These practices shaped her life. She contracted smallpox and died in her twentieth year. This adapted prayer is taken from her journal entries just prior to her death.

Hymn:

In the bleak midwinter, frosty wind made moan,
earth stood hard as iron, water like a stone;
snow had fallen, snow on snow, snow on snow,

in the bleak midwinter, long ago.

Our God, heaven cannot hold him, nor earth sustain;
heaven and earth shall flee away when he comes to reign.
In the bleak midwinter a stable place sufficed
the Lord God Almighty, Jesus Christ.

Angels and archangels may have gathered there,
cherubim and seraphim thronged the air;
but his mother only, in her maiden bliss,
worshiped the beloved with a kiss.

What can I give him, poor as I am?
If I were a shepherd, I would bring a lamb;
if I were a Wise Man, I would do my part;
yet what I can I give him: give my heart.

—UMH 221 (Christina Rossetti)

Christina Rossetti (1830–1894) received her education in an Italian home characterized by its culture and art. When her family emigrated to England, she became a devout Anglican. She was a prolific composer of devotional and poetic writings, her hymns still considered to be among the most beautiful examples of lyrical eloquence in any hymnbook.

Engage:

When did you first give your heart to Jesus, and what does that mean to you now?

Reflections:

9

Love Came Down

Scripture:

Beloved, let us love one another, because love is from God; everyone who loves is born of God and knows God. Whoever does not love does not know God, for God is love. God's love was revealed among us in this way: God sent his only Son into the world so that we might live through him. In this is love, not that we loved God but that he loved us and sent his Son to be the atoning sacrifice for our sins. Beloved, since God loved us so much, we also ought to love one another. No one has ever seen God; if we love one another, God lives in us, and his love is perfected in us.

—1 John 4:7–12

Prayer:

O my blessed Lord,
    you have demonstrated your love to me over and over again,
        and you continue to sustain my soul by your grace and love.
How can I do anything other than put my whole trust in you
    when you have dealt with me in such a loving way?

I can never sufficiently praise your holy name.
    Your love is unspeakable!
       Your delight is to make us happy.
          Oh, how this love exceeds all I could imagine.
My soul cries out, "I have heard great and glorious things spoken
    about you,
    but, oh, how little was said to what I find!"
I cannot even begin to express the joy I feel because I am united
    with you!
    I rejoice in your redeeming love.
       You are most precious and altogether lovely.
You are my good physician.
    You do all things well.
       You are the lover of my soul.
You came to my relief.
    You shed your precious blood because of your love for me.
       Because of your great love, you reign with God in glory.
Love came down in you, O Jesus, and revealed the true God of light.
    Let your love shine in my heart forever. Amen

                              —Isabella Wilson, *Diary*

Hymn:

Love came down at Christmas, Love all lovely, Love divine;
Love was born at Christmas; star and angels gave the sign.
Worship we the Godhead, Love incarnate, Love divine;
worship we our Jesus, but wherewith for sacred sign?
Love shall be our token; love be yours and love be mine;
love to God and all men, love for plea and gift and sign.

                     —UMH 242 (Christina Rossetti)

Engage:

What does it mean to you when you sing, "Love came down at Christmas?"

Reflections:

10

Redemption in Christ

Scripture:

In him we have redemption through his blood, the forgiveness of our trespasses, according to the riches of his grace that he lavished on us. With all wisdom and insight he has made known to us the mystery of his will, according to his good pleasure that he set forth in Christ, as a plan for the fullness of time, to gather up all things in him, things in heaven and things on earth.

—Ephesians 1:7–10

Prayer:

O God of my redemption,
I have so many reasons to adore, to praise,
    to magnify your goodness and love
        for sending your Son into the world
            to die for me and all who have sinned.
I have so many reasons to praise and adore
    and love your Son who suffered so much
        to redeem me from the bondage of my sin!

Such boundless love to souls!
    I have no means by which to express
        the depths of my gratitude.
Gladly and cheerfully I take up my cross
        for him who suffered death upon the cross for me!
I praise and adore the blessed Spirit
    who sanctifies and illuminates my soul,
        who offers the grace of my Lord, Jesus Christ,
            through the instruments of prayer, and Scripture,
            and the holy meal.
You condescend, my God, to visit and assist and refresh my soul
    through the powerful influences of your present Spirit.
Glory be to the Father! Son! and Holy Spirit!
    For on the cross Jesus revealed the true nature
        of your redemptive love and mercy
            and the way in which you offer it to me
                and to all your beloved children. Amen.

—Susanna Wesley, *Writings*

Susanna Wesley (1669–1742) was the precocious daughter of Samuel Annesley, one of the great Puritan preachers in London toward the end of the seventeenth century. After her marriage to Samuel Wesley, the couple raised their large family at Epworth, a country parish in Lincolnshire. She is remembered, not because she was a theologian of high caliber to be reckoned with, but as the mother of John and Charles Wesley, co-founders of Methodism. This "mother of Methodism" expounded the doctrinal themes of Puritanism and Anglicanism in her prolific writings.

Hymn:

O Morning Star, how fair and bright
thou beamest forth in truth and light,
O Sovereign meek and lowly!
Thou Root of Jesse, David's Son,

my Lord and Master, thou has won
my heart to serve thee solely!
Thou art holy,
fair and glorious, all-victorious,
rich in blessing,
rule and might o'er all possessing.

Thou heavenly Brightness! Light divine!
O deep within my heart now shine,
and make thee there an altar!
fill me with joy and strength to be
thy member, ever joined to thee
in love that cannot falter;
toward thee longing
doth possess me; turn and bless me;
here in sadness
eye and heart long for thy gladness.

—UMH 247 (trans. Catherine Winkworth)

Engage:

What does the phrase "redemption in Christ" mean to you?

Reflections:

11

A Song of Gladness

Scripture:

Jesus said to her, "I am the resurrection and the life. Those who believe in me, even though they die, will live, and everyone who lives and believes in me will never die. Do you believe this?" She said to him, "Yes, Lord, I believe that you are the Messiah, the Son of God, the one coming into the world."

—John 11:25–27

Prayer:

Christ the Lord is risen today!
    In flowers that burst through winter's snow
        and promise new life in the midst of death.
    They fill our hearts with gladness. Alleluia!
Christ the Lord is risen today!
    In a multitude of blessings that fill our lives with
        love and laughter, joy and peace.
    They raise us above the agonies of life. Alleluia!
Christ the Lord is risen today!

In a steadfast love that knows no bounds,
    that bears us up and keeps us free.
It abides in our hearts to keep them strong and true. Alleluia!
Christ the Lord is risen today!
In a present, living Lord who came to save,
    who breaks the power of sin and death.
You free us from the darkness of the grave
    and fill our hearts with courage
        so we can be your agents of love in the world. Alleluia!

—Georgia Harkness, *Grace Abounding*

Georgia Harkness (1891–1974) served as the first female professor in a major theological seminary in the United States. In 1947, she was named one of the ten most influential living Methodists in the world. A prolific author, her theological writings and her hymns (both featured in this volume) reflect the concerns of her Personalist heritage: continuity, experience, optimism, social justice, and truth-seeking—all centered in a vital relationship with God through Christ. The style of her thought was generous, tolerant, and wide-ranging.

Hymn:

In thee is gladness, amid all sadness,
Jesus, sunshine of my heart.
By thee are given the gifts of heaven,
thou the true Redeemer art.
Our souls thou makest, our bonds thou breakest;
who trusts thee surely hath built securely,
and stands forever. Alleluia!
Our hearts are pining to see thy shining;
dying or living, to thee are cleaving;
naught can us sever. Alleluia!

If God be ours, we fear no powers,

not of earth or sin or death.
God sees and blesses in worst distresses,
and can change them in a breath.
Wherefore the story tell of God's glory
with heart and voices; all heaven rejoices,
singing forever; Alleluia!
We shout for gladness, triumph o'er sadness,
loving and praising, voices still raising
glad hymns forever: Alleluia!

—UMH 169 (trans. Catherine Winkworth)

Engage:

Describe a time when you experienced "resurrection" in your
own life.

Reflections:

PART 3

The Power of the Holy Spirit

An Introductory Comment

The devotions of this section focus on the Holy Spirit—the third person of the Trinity. The women placed the Spirit at the very center of their understanding of the Christian life. It is through the gracious presence and power of the Spirit that all people come to know who God is, are restored in their relationship with God, and develop those virtues, or fruits, that characterize the children of God. The prayers and hymns in this section explore the dimensions of the Spirit's work in repentance, conversion, and assurance—all those actions that elicit our praise and blessing of God.

12

The Penitent Heart

Scripture:

Repent therefore, and turn to God so that your sins may be wiped out, so that times of refreshing may come from the presence of the Lord.

—Acts 3:19–20a

Prayer:

Lord, do you care for me?
  Am I able to cast all my cares, even all my sins upon you?
May I? Do you bid me to do this?
  A poor sinner—a sinner against light
    and conviction and repeated vows?
Can such love dwell in you? Is it not too easy a way?
May I, even I, be saved, if I only cast my soul on Jesus?
  My burden of sin, my load of guilt, my every crime?
What, saved from all this guilt?
  Saved into the favor of God! the holy God!
    and become God's child, and that now, this moment!

O it is too great!
Lord Jesus, I will, I do believe.
I now venture my whole salvation upon you as God!
I put my guilty soul into your hands;
Your blood is sufficient!
I cast my soul upon you for all time and eternity. Amen.

—Hester Ann Rogers, *Experience*

Hymn:

Pass me not, O gentle Savior,
hear my humble cry;
while on others thou art calling,
do not pass me by.
Refrain:
Savior, Savior, hear my humble cry;
while on others thou art calling,
do not pass me by.

Let me at thy throne of mercy
find a sweet relief,
kneeling there in deep contrition;
help my unbelief.
(*Refrain*)

Thou the spring of all my comfort,
more than life to me,
whom have I on earth beside thee?
Whom in heaven but thee?
(*Refrain*)

—UMH 351:1–2, 4 (Fanny Crosby)

Engage:

How do you feel when you don't think you deserve the spiritual blessings you receive?

Reflections:

13

God's Saving Grace

Scripture:

Therefore just as one man's trespass led to condemnation for all, so one man's act of righteousness leads to justification and life for all. For just as by the one man's disobedience the many were made sinners, so by the one man's obedience the many will be made righteous. Just as sin exercised dominion in death, so grace might also exercise dominion through justification leading to eternal life through Jesus Christ our Lord.

—Romans 5:18–19, 21

Prayer:

O gracious and adorable Being!
    Look with compassion on a soul
        which pants for grace and forgiveness!
    A soul sensible of her weak and broken state
        and relying entirely on your mercy and grace.
O gracious and adorable Being!
    Give me a new heart and a new spirit

freed from the burden of sin and grief!
A soul elevated by your grace and peace
    and sensible of your original design of love.
O gracious and adorable Being!
  Heal the wounds I have inflicted upon myself
    through my proud and selfish actions.
A soul pardoned, cleansed, liberated
    and now longing to see you face to face.
O gracious and adorable Being!
  hear and grant my prayer,
    for the sake of Jesus Christ.
  Your grace flows through him—
    my only Mediator and Redeemer. Amen.

—Mrs. Lefevre, *Letters*

Mrs. Lefevre (1722–1756) exerted an incalculable influence upon a number of important early Methodist women, to say nothing of the high esteem in which she was held by the leadership of the Wesleyan movement. It is unfortunate, indeed, that we know so little about this remarkable woman. Her celebrated *Letters upon Sacred Subjects*, published a year after her death by her husband, reveal the depth of her piety, the wisdom beyond her years, and her tremendous gifts as a spiritual guide and friend. These letters made her famous within Methodist circles.

Hymn:

Beneath the cross of Jesus
I fain would take my stand,
the shadow of a mighty rock
within a weary land;
a home within the wilderness,
a rest upon the way,
from the burning of the noontide heat,
and the burden of the day.

Upon that cross of Jesus
mine eye at times can see
the very dying form of One
who suffered there for me;
and from my stricken heart with tears
two wonders I confess:
the wonders of redeeming love
and my unworthiness.

I take, O cross, thy shadow
for my abiding place;
I ask no other sunshine than
the sunshine of his face;
content to let the world go by,
to know no gain nor loss,
my sinful self my only shame,
my glory all the cross.

—UMH 297 (Elizabeth Clephane)

Elizabeth Clephane (1830–1869) was renowned for her kindness and generosity to the poor in the Scottish Borders, south of Edinburgh. Her hymn-writing emerged from her concern for families. The hymn featured here, "Beneath the Cross of Jesus," is the most famous from a collection of eight of her compositions published in *The Family Treasury*.

Engage:

The word "grace" appears eight times in the hymn above. How do you define grace?

Reflections:

14

Blessed Assurance

Scripture:

Come to me, all you that are weary and are carrying heavy burdens, and I will give you rest. Take my yoke upon you, and learn from me; for I am gentle and humble in heart, and you will find rest for your souls. For my yoke is easy, and my burden is light.

—Matthew 11:28–30

Prayer:

O compassionate Savior,
   you speak words of rest and assurance to me;
      you call and I obey.
I come unto you for rest, peace, and everlasting refreshment.
   Wearied from following the paths of folly and vanity,
      wearied with deceitful hopes and idle fears,
         I come to you for peace and blessed assurance.
I find that assurance in your promises;
   your promises are truth itself.
      Heaven and earth shall pass away,

but your word shall never fail.
So I come to you for peace and blessed assurance.
Oh save me from myself! Oh give me that rest!
Oh offer me that blessed assurance!
Then shall all be perfect peace and harmony,
and my soul shall feel no emotions
but those of joy and gratitude, eternal gratitude
for my gracious and almighty benefactor,
to whom I come for peace and blessed assurance. Amen.

—Mrs. Lefevre, *Letters*

Hymn:

Blessed assurance, Jesus is mine!
O what a foretaste of glory divine!
Heir of salvation, purchase of God,
born of his Spirit, washed in his blood.
Refrain:
This is my story, this is my song,
praising my Savior all the day long;
this is my story, this is my song,
praising my Savior all the day long.

Perfect submission, perfect delight,
visions of rapture now burst on my sight;
angels descending bring from above
echoes of mercy, whispers of love.
(*Refrain*)

Perfect submission, all is at rest;
I in my Savior am happy and blest,
watching and waiting, looking above,
filled with his goodness, lost in his love.
(*Refrain*)

—UMH 369 (Fanny Crosby)

Engage:

How does your sense of assurance shape your day-to-day life?

Reflections:

PART 4

Holiness of Heart and Life

An Introductory Comment

It should be no surprise that the largest section of this volume provides prayers and hymns related to holiness of heart and life. The spirituality of these women focuses, more than anything else, on how one lives, and they anchor their vision in the idea of holiness as love filling the heart. This book takes its title from this section. Holiness begins with our desire for peace and the way in which humility shapes this gift. These prayers and hymns elevate the need to be close to God and to conform to God's vision. This intimacy requires open eyes and open hearts to God's rule and way—God's love and stillness.

15

Close to You

Scripture:

> The eyes of all look to you,
>> and you give them their food in due season.
> You open your hand,
>> satisfying the desire of every living thing.
> The Lord is just in all his ways,
>> and kind in all his doings.
> The Lord is near to all who call on him,
>> to all who call on him in truth.
>
> —Psalm 145:15–18

Prayer:

O Almighty Lord and Savior,
  I renew my covenant with you with heart-felt joy.
May your Holy Spirit guide me
  through this pilgrimage of life to the heavenly Canaan.
O my Lord, I pass with delight through the wilderness of this world,
  for the light of your countenance shines upon me daily.

O my God, it is enough.
I reflect on you and your fire burns within me;
> but, oh, in what language shall the flame break forth?
> What can I say but this:
> > "My heart admires you, adores you, and loves you?"
My little vessel is as full as it can hold,
> and I would pour out all that fullness before you,
> > that my heart may become capable of receiving more and more.
You are my hope, and help, and salvation.
O blessed Lord, let the dew of your grace fall on me continually,
> then I will not fail to flourish as willows by flowing waters.
May I walk humbly with you, my God,
> all the days of my life,
> > that I may at last rise to life immortal. Amen.

—Isabella Wilson, *Diary*

Hymn:

Thou my everlasting portion,
more than friend or life to me,
all along my pilgrim journey,
Savior, let me walk with thee.

Refrain:
Close to thee, close to thee,
close to thee, close to thee,
all along my pilgrim journey,
Savior, let me walk with thee.

Lead me through the vale of shadows,
bear me o'er life's fitful sea;
then the gate of life eternal
may I enter, Lord, with thee.

(*Refrain*)

—UMH 407:1, 3 (Fanny Crosby)

Engage:

When have you felt most close to the Lord during the past week?

Reflections:

16

Draw Me Nearer

Scripture:

May the God of peace himself sanctify you entirely; and may your spirit and soul and body be kept sound and blameless at the coming of our Lord Jesus Christ. The one who calls you is faithful, and he will do this.

—1 Thessalonians 5:23-24

Prayer:

Come, Lord Jesus, come quickly,
    and conform my life to that which you lived!
Burn up, O Spirit of burning, all the dross of my best intentions—
    all the stubble of my inbred sin!
O my lovely Jesus, I languish to be all holy,
    according to my degree, as you are holy.
I beseech you, come quickly to destroy the very in-being of sin
    which holds me back from loving and praising you
        as I ardently long to do!
When, O my dear Redeemer, when shall I enjoy

that heaven of loving you alone?
   I pant for more of the divine life—
   I thirst for a full salvation from sin.
   I reach up to the fullest possible love—
   I hunger for that sacred spark of love divine.
   I yearn for your love to glow in my longing breast—
   I await the overflowing cup of your soul-transporting love.
      Thy only love to me be given—
      Lord, I ask no other heaven. Amen.

                       —Margaret Davidson, *Life*

Margaret Davidson (d. 1780), the first Methodist woman preacher in Ireland, was born into a poor family near Killinchy and blinded by an attack of small pox at two years of age. She was held in high esteem in the community for her ministry of prayer. Margaret contributed greatly to a significant revival that took place in Ballinderry where she began open-air preaching. Her preaching style reflects the unique nature of her spirituality, holding the Anglican prayer book in one hand and the Methodist hymn book in the other. Her central theme was love for Jesus.

Hymn:

I am thine, O Lord, I have heard thy voice,
and it told thy love to me;
but I long to rise in the arms of faith
and be closer drawn to thee.
Refrain:
Draw me nearer, nearer, blessed Lord,
to the cross where thou hast died.
Draw me nearer, nearer, nearer, blessed Lord,
to thy precious, bleeding side.

Consecrate me now to thy service, Lord,
by the power of grace divine;

let my soul look up with a steadfast hope,
and my will be lost in thine.
(*Refrain*)

There are depths of love that I cannot know
till I cross the narrow sea;
there are heights of joy that I may not reach
till I rest in peace with thee.
(*Refrain*)

—UMH 419:1–2, 4 (Fanny Crosby)

Engage:

Which of the following—pant, thirst, hunger, yearn, await—best describes you? Why?

Reflections:

17

A Blessed Vision

Scripture:

Blessed are those who hunger and thirst for righteousness, for
they will be filled.
Blessed are the merciful, for they will receive mercy.
Blessed are the pure in heart, for they will see God.
Blessed are the peacemakers, for they will be called children of
God.

—Matthew 5:6–9

Prayer:

God of light and love, justice and compassion!
Wherever your gospel is preached and received,
    you set up your beloved community in that place.
Whenever anyone embraces Christ
    and the glad tidings of salvation,
    you set up your beloved community in that person's heart.
        Blessed are those who receive and embrace your rule.
Blessedness consists in righteousness, peace, and joy,

all begun in redemption but fulfilled in restoration.
Blessed are those you fill with understanding and light,
 who have discovered that you love everyone
 and yearn to gather all nations to yourself.
  Blessed are those who receive and embrace your rule.
Whenever we strive for holiness of heart and life,
 you cleanse us from all unrighteousness.
Whenever we embrace your way and your will,
 you establish your rule in our hearts and communities,
 melting away all anger and strife, all hunger and pain.
  Blessed are those who receive and embrace your rule.
Put your Spirit within us, O God,
 that we might walk in your way
  and love you with all our hearts. Amen.

—Hester Ann Rogers, *Experience*

Hymn:

Be thou my vision, O Lord of my heart;
naught be all else to me, save that thou art.
Thou my best thought, by day or by night,
waking or sleeping, thy presence my light.

Be thou my wisdom, and thou my true word;
I ever with thee and thou with me, Lord;
thou and thou only, first in my heart,
great God of heaven, my treasure thou art.

Great God of heaven, my victory won,
may I reach heaven's joys, O bright heaven's Sun!
Heart of my own heart, whatever befall,
still be my vision, O Ruler of all.

—UMH 451 (trans. Mary E. Byrne)

Mary E. Byrne [Máiri Ní Bhroin] (1880–1931) was born and educated in Dublin. An educator dedicated to her native culture and literature, she engaged in research and publication to keep the traditions of Ireland alive. The hymn featured here is her famous translation of the eighth-century "Rop tú ma baile a Choimdhiu cride."

Engage:

What characteristic of Jesus and his ministry shapes your vision of life most fully?

Reflections:

18

The Kingdom Around and Within

Scripture:

> Pray then in this way:
> Our Father in heaven,
>   hallowed be your name.
> Your kingdom come.
>   Your will be done,
>   on earth as it is in heaven.

> —Matthew 6:8–10

Prayer:

O God of the world around us;
  God of the strange world within us—
    Help us to yield ourselves to you.
  Purge us of pride, self-will, and anxiety;
    stir us anew to rest in you.
  For so shall the souls of all your children be restored
    and our world brought nearer to your good design.
O God of the world around us;

God of the strange world within us—
  Help us to be still and know that you are God.
In the stillness we hear you speak
  through the sounds of your undisturbed world.
Our souls are restored as they commune with you
  and the world resonates anew with the harmony of love.
O God of the world around us;
  God of the strange world within us—
  Help us to live under your peaceable reign.
You are both the life-giving sun that warms us
  and the son of righteousness who heals us.
May we ever, by our living and our speaking,
  Embrace our role as your agents in your world.
By our working and our living,
  may we render grateful praise to you
  for the worlds that you have made. Amen.

—Georgia Harkness, *Grace Abounding*

Hymn:

What gift can we bring, what present, what token?
What words can convey it, the joy of this day?
When grateful we come, remembering, rejoicing,
what song can we offer in honor and praise?

Give thanks for the past, for those who had vision,
who planted and watered so dreams could come true.
Give thanks for the now, for study, for worship,
for mission that bids us turn prayer into deed.

Give thanks for tomorrow, full of surprises,
for knowing whatever tomorrow may bring,
the Word is our promise always, forever,
we rest in God's keeping and live in God's love.

—UMH 87:1–3 (Jane Marshall)

Jane Marshall (1924–2019) received the coveted Roger N. Deschner Award for "outstanding contributions to the music and worship life of the church" in 1997. This "commemorative hymn," composed in Dallas in 1980, strikes Marshall's signature keynote of gratitude, a theme cultivated in the hearts of faithful people principally, she believed, through their singing.

Engage:

What gift do you feel God calling you to develop more fully and offer for Christ's sake?

Reflections:

19

Open Eyes; Open Hearts

Scripture:

O the depth of the riches and wisdom and knowledge of God!
How unsearchable are his judgments and how inscrutable his
ways!
"For who has known the mind of the Lord?
Or who has been his counselor?"
"Or who has given a gift to him,
to receive a gift in return?"
For from him and through him and to him are all things. To him
be the glory forever. Amen.

—Romans 11:33–36

Prayer:

God of creativity and love,
open our eyes to the treasures of your diverse family.
Help us to celebrate the gifts of all your children.
Banish our arrogance and tribalism;
help us to prize what you have given us,

to honor what we see in others,
and to work together for a world of freedom,
equality, and justice for all.
God of compassion and grace,
open our hands to the needs of a suffering world.
Help us to care for the vulnerable and marginalized.
Banish our complacency and thoughtlessness;
help us to discern our duty,
to speak and to act with courage
in the service of all people
and the realization of your blessed rule.
God of vision and mission,
open our minds to the idea of your peaceable reign.
Help us to cultivate the values of your realm.
Banish our prejudice and animosity;
help us to go forward, loving you and all people,
obeying your call and embodying
your will and your way
in the healing of the world. Amen.

—Georgia Harkness, *Grace Abounding*

Hymn:

Open my eyes, that I may see
glimpses of truth thou hast for me;
place in my hands the wonderful key
that shall unclasp and set me free.
Silently now I wait for thee,
ready, my God, thy will to see.
Open my eyes, illumine me, Spirit divine!

Open my mouth, and let me bear
gladly the warm truth everywhere;
open my heart and let me prepare

love with thy children thus to share.
Silently now I wait for thee,
ready, my God, thy will to see.
Open my heart, illumine me, Spirit divine!

—UMH 454:1, 3 (Clara Scott)

Clara Scott (1841–1897), a prolific composer of both music and
lyrics, was born in Chicago where she studied at the C. M. Cady
Music Institute. She produced what is thought to be the first collection of anthems published by a woman in the United States.
The selection featured here first appeared in a collection of hymns,
entitled *Truth in Song,* in 1896.

Engage:

Where did you catch a sighting of God today and what did it do
to you?

Reflections:

20

The Lord's Speech

Scripture:

We do not live to ourselves, and we do not die to ourselves. If we live, we live to the Lord, and if we die, we die to the Lord; so then, whether we live or whether we die, we are the Lord's. For to this end Christ died and lived again, so that he might be Lord of both the dead and the living.

—Romans 14:7–9

Prayer:

Lord, you speak these words to me,
  "I am the resurrection and the life,"
    and you flood my soul with light and joy and love.
  I find my whole heart—
    all my affections—
      firmly fixed on you, O Lord.
  I have no will but yours,
    no happiness but in doing what you command.
Lord, you speak these words to me,

"I am the good shepherd,"
and my soul rests upon your bosom—my Beloved.
I pray from my inmost being,
that I will be able to proclaim
the wonders of your love.
I have no voice but yours,
so put your words in my heart and on my lips.
Lord, you speak these words to me,
"I am the light of the world,"
and I long for others to see your light in me.
Help me to die to self, therefore, so I can live to you.
Let my speech always be gracious,
so that I may be a winsome witness for you.
To you be honor, glory, majesty, and dominion,
now and for evermore. Amen.

—Sarah Ryan, *Account*

Sarah Ryan (1724–1768) was one of John Wesley's most intimate correspondents. She was converted to Methodism under the preaching of George Whitefield in London in the early 1740s and became an active member of Wesley's original Foundery Society. Sarah joined Mary Bosanquet in her benevolent activities in London and became her close companion in the years that followed. Sarah mentored a large circle of women who modeled their lives after her dynamic combination of interior personal piety and active social service.

Hymn:

Lord, speak to me, that I may speak
in living echoes of thy tone;
as thou has sought, so let me seek
thine erring children lost and lone.

O strengthen me, that while I stand

firm on the rock, and strong in thee,
I may stretch out a loving land
to wrestlers with the troubled sea.

O teach me, Lord, that I may teach
the precious things thou dost impart;
and wing my words, that they may reach
the hidden depths of many a heart.

—UMH 463:1–3 (Frances Havergal)

Frances Havergal (1836–1879), inherited a lyrical gift from her father, an Anglican priest noted for his hymns. A precocious and religious child, she became a remarkable musician and linguist. In 1873, she experienced what she described as "full surrender" to God and composed the selection here—"Consecration Hymn"—as an act of commitment.

Engage:

In the prayer above, Jesus speaks particular words to us. Which mean the most to you?

Reflections:

21

Filled with Love

Scripture:

God abides in those who confess that Jesus is the Son of God, and
they abide in God. So we have known and believe the love that
God has for us. God is love, and those who abide in love abide in
God, and God abides in them.

—1 John 4:15–16

Prayer:

O blessed fountain of love,
    fill my heart more with your divine principle!
Sink me lower in the depths of humility,
    and let me sit at your feet
        and learn from you.
May your love fill my heart, as the Scripture expresses it,
    "the love of God, shed abroad in your hearts
        by the Holy Ghost, given unto you."
If I get my heart full of your love, O God,
    I know that this will be the oil

by which the lamp of faith will be ever kept burning.
I pray much, O God, for this love;
and I remember your word,
"Those who dwell in love
dwell in God, and God in them!"
Enlarge my soul that I may better contemplate
your glory and your love.
May I prove myself your child
by bearing a resemblance to you,
my heavenly Father! Amen.

—Mary Tooth, *Account*

Mary Tooth (1777–1843) is known almost exclusively because of her connections with the famous Methodist preacher, Mary Fletcher. A large collection of their letters is preserved in the Methodist Archives in Manchester, England. Perhaps a native of Shropshire, she exhibited an early concern for the religious life. Mary became a strong proponent of women in ministry and engaged in preaching herself as late as the 1830s. She provided the account of Mary Fletcher's death, from which this adapted prayer was drawn.

Hymn:

O fill me with thy fullness, Lord,
until my very heart o'erflow
in kindling thought and glowing word,
thy love to tell, thy praise to show.

O use me, Lord, use even me,
just as thou wilt, and when, and where,
until thy blessed face I see,
thy rest, thy joy, thy glory share.

—UMH 463:4–5 (Frances Havergal)

Engage:

Describe a time in which you felt absolutely filled with God's love.

Reflections:

22

Come Near

Scripture:

Jesus said to [the Samaritan woman], "Everyone who drinks of this water will be thirsty again, but those who drink of the water that I will give them will never be thirsty. The water that I will give will become in them a spring of water gushing up to eternal life." The woman said to him, "Sir, give me this water, so that I may never be thirsty or have to keep coming here to draw water."

—John 4:13–15

Prayer:

Savior of sinners!
When a poor, outcast woman of Samaria
    went out to the well to draw water,
        she found you sitting there, waiting for her.
    She had not sought you,
        but you were ready to give her
            that blessing which she had never sought.
    Jesus, you are in the midst of us;

You are near to us, know us, and love us all!
Lord, you are with your people still.
We see you in the middle of the night,
    when we toss and turn with worry and doubt.
You are near to those who do not know you.
    Open their eyes so they can see that you are near,
        extending your invitation, "Come unto me."
Jesus, you are in the midst of us;
You are near to us, know us, and love us all!
We long to be near to you, O Lord,
    like the woman at the well,
        transform us through your abiding love. Amen.

—Elizabeth Evans, *Adam Bede*

Elizabeth Evans (1776–1849) was the niece of the famous novelist George Eliot (aka Mary Ann Evans). Elizabeth's biography and the story of Eliot's fictional Dinah Morris, heroine of *Adam Bede*, are so inextricably bound together that it is virtually impossible to separate them. She continued to conduct evangelistic tours even after restrictions were placed on Methodist women in 1803. While Elizabeth Evans's sermons have been lost, this one prayer was passed on carefully through her husband and found its way into *Adam Bede*, on the lips of Dinah Morris.

Hymn:

Nearer, my God, to thee, nearer to thee!
E'en though it be a cross that raiseth me,
still all my song shall be,
nearer, my God, to thee;
nearer, my God, to thee, nearer to thee!

Though like the wanderer, the sun gone down,
darkness be over me, my rest a stone;
yet in my dreams I'd be

nearer, my God, to thee;
nearer, my God, to thee, nearer to thee!

Then, with my waking thoughts bright with thy praise,
out of my stony griefs Bethel I'll raise;
so by my woes to be
nearer, my God, to thee;
nearer, my God, to thee, nearer to thee!

—UMH 528:1-2, 4 (Sarah Adams)

Sarah Adams (1805–1848) was a member of the Unitarian chapel at Finsbury in London. She was a friend of Robert Browning in his youth. Sarah may even have been the model for his heroine in *Pauline* (1833). In addition to her own poetry, Sarah published a catechetical book for children that included hymns, the source of this particular selection.

Engage:

In what ways do you related to the Samaritan woman at the well with Jesus?

Reflections:

23

Be Still, and Know

Scripture:

> "Be still, and know that I am God!
> I am exalted among the nations,
> I am exalted in the earth."
> The LORD of hosts is with us;
> the God of Jacob is our refuge.

—Psalm 46:10–11

Prayer:

Blessed Lord,
   You know the one desire of my heart.
      You have done so much for me!
         My gratitude overflows for such deliverance!
   Lord, make me pure, spiritual, and holy.
      Mold this passive clay as you will.
   I want to live sweetly and quietly in your will
      and prove that you—my God—are love.
Blessed Lord,

You are the one glory of my life.
     Let me begin afresh to bless you!
          I freely offer myself to you.
     Guide me by your wisdom, for I am yours,
          and instruct me by your Spirit.
     You have accepted me just as I am;
          keep me at your feet till you receive me at last.
Blessed Lord,
     You offer me the one joy of my soul.
          Help me to share freely the gift of your love!
          I long to possess a greater fullness of your Spirit.
     Let me rest quietly in your loving arms;
          align my will with yours in all things.
     Quiet my soul, O Lord, and teach me
          that you are always with me—my refuge and my God.
Amen.

—Sarah Crosby, *Account*

Sarah Crosby (1729–1804) was the first woman preacher of Methodism and a formidable influence with regard to early Methodist spirituality. Her intimate connection with the Leytonstone Circle of Women in London located her in a strategic center of women's activities in the Wesleyan revival. She embodied John Wesley's goal of holiness of heart and life—love for God and all people. She afforded primary leadership for the so-called "Female Brethren" in Leeds. Her *Account* consists of meditation on her spiritual experience of abiding in Christ.

Hymn:

Be still, my soul: the Lord is on your side.
Bear patiently the cross of grief or pain;
leave to your God to order and provide;
in every change God faithful will remain.
Be still, my soul: your best, your heavenly friend

through thorny ways leads to a joyful end.

Be still, my soul: your God will undertake
to guide the future, as in ages past.
Your hope, your confidence let nothing shake;
all now mysterious shall be bright at last.
Be still, my soul: the waves and winds still know
the Christ who ruled them while he dwelt below.

Be still, my soul: the hour is hastening on
when we shall be forever with the Lord,
when disappointment, grief, and fear are gone,
sorrow forgot, love's purest joys restored.
Be still, my soul: when change and tears are past,
all safe and blessed we shall meet at last.

—UMH 534 (trans. Jane Borthwick)

Jane Borthwick (1813–1897), a staunch member of the Free Church of Scotland, collaborated with her sister, Sarah Findlater, in the production of *Hymns from the Land of Luther*. Included in this volume was the hymn of another woman—an early eighteenth-century Lutheran Pietiest, Katharina von Schlegel—now made more famous by Jane's English translation.

Engage:

What is disturbing the stillness of your soul today? How can you lay it at Jesus' feet?

Reflections:

24

Precious Name

Scripture:

An angel of the Lord appeared to him in a dream and said, "Joseph, son of David, do not be afraid to take Mary as your wife, for the child conceived in her is from the Holy Spirit. She will bear a son, and you are to name him Jesus, for he will save his people from their sins."

—Matthew 1:20b–21

Prayer:

O my precious Jesus,
   I am not worthy to come under your roof.
      Teach me to praise you for all your mercies.
O my precious Jesus,
   let me weep and love much because I have been much forgiven.
      Let me sit at your feet and wait till you fully heal my soul.
O my precious Jesus,
   be the rock that shall cover me in that great day.
      May I find sanctuary in your wounds.

O my precious Jesus,
> whatever I suffer, let me not turn away from you.
> Be glorified in my salvation and not in my destruction.

O my precious Jesus,
> hasten the time when I shall taste and see you.
> In all that I do, may my heart be always with you.

O my precious Jesus,
> Help me to be your faithful servant and prosper my labor.
> Keep my eye fixed on your glory.

O my precious Jesus,
> Open my eyes that I may see your footsteps.
> Keep me in the path that leads to life eternal. Amen.

—Susannah Design, Manuscript Journal

Susannah Design (fl. 1740s) left behind a forty-three-page manuscript journal, the only source of information concerning the life of this early Methodist woman. She prepared this narrative account of her religious experience for Charles Wesley at his request in 1742. She was a leader of the Methodist Society in Bristol during its most formative decade and was acutely concerned about her spiritual well-being. Susannah punctuates the narrative with brief prayers articulating her earnest longing for purity of heart and extolling the precious nature of life in Christ.

Hymn:

Take the name of Jesus with you,
child of sorrow and of woe;
it will joy and comfort give you;
take it then, where'er you go.
Refrain:
Precious name, O how sweet!
Hope of earth and joy of heaven.
Precious name, O how sweet!
Hope of earth and joy of heaven.

O the precious name of Jesus!
How it thrills our souls with joy,
when his loving arms receive us,
and his songs our tongues employ!
(*Refrain*)

At the name of Jesus bowing,
falling prostrate at his feet,
King of kings in heaven we'll crown him,
when our journey is complete.
(*Refrain*)

—UMH 536:1, 3–4 (Lydia Baxter)

Lydia Baxter (1809–1874) was a formidable gospel song writer and native of New York. Converted under the preaching of Baptist missionary Eben Tucker, she helped establish a Baptist church in Petersburg. Despite her invalid condition in her adult years, Lydia's home remained a base for evangelistic campaigns, such as those led by Dwight Moody and Ira Sankey.

Engage:

The prayer addresses Jesus as "precious." What is most precious to you about the Lord?

Reflections:

PART 5

The Community of Faith

An Introductory Comment

The women's writings in this final part of the volume elevate the importance of community. Family life involves a pilgrimage in which we walk together toward a goal. The prayers and hymns of the women here describe the various dimensions of the church—the community of faith. The goal toward which we move is perfect love and the realization of God's great vision for all creation. The women view death as a portal leading to life eternal and the celebration of God's victory of love with all the saints.

25

Heralds of the Lord

Scripture:

> O God, when you went out before your people,
>> when you marched through the wilderness, *Selah*
> the earth quaked, the heavens poured down rain
>> at the presence of God, the God of Sinai,
>> at the presence of God, the God of Israel.
> Rain in abundance, O God, you showered abroad;
>> you restored your heritage when it languished;
> your flock found a dwelling in it;
>> in your goodness, O God, you provided for the needy.
> The Lord gives the command;
>> great is the company of the women who bore the tidings.
>
> —Psalm 68:7–11

Prayer:

My gracious Parent,
> No language can describe my gratitude to you.
>> You see my heart and that suffices you,

knowing my delight is in you, my God, my Life.
I will always herald your joyful praise
and testify to your love and goodness to all.
Enable me to finish well the work you have given me to do.
May my proclamation of your blessedness
win the hearts of many, as they claimed my heart.
O, that I could tell a hundredth part of your love
in which you have loved the world and all your children.
May everyone hear of your glory through my testimony.
May everyone believe you worthy of praise
because of the witness of my life.
May everyone embrace the truth of your love
because I have been faithful
in heralding your message to the world.
As the endless ages roll round,
keep my heart and mind ever open
to new scenes of wonder, love, and grace. Amen.

—Dorothy Ripley, *Account*

Hymn:

Heralds of Christ, who bear the King's commands,
immortal tidings in your mortal hands,
pass on and carry swift the news you bring;
make straight, make straight the highway of the King.

Through desert ways, dark fen, and deep morass,
through jungles, sluggish seas, and mountain pass,
build now the road, and falter not, nor stay;
prepare across the earth the King's highway.

Lord, give us faith and strength the road to build,
to see the promise of the day fulfilled,

when war shall be no more, and strife shall cease
upon the highway of the Prince of Peace.

—UMH 567 (Laura Copenhaver)

Laura Copenhaver (1868–1940), the daughter of a Lutheran minister from Texas, started teaching Sunday School when she was ten years of age. An educator throughout her life, Laura's primary interests revolved around literature and poetry and how these might be used in mission. She founded Rosemont Industries to improve the lives of dispossessed children in Appalachia.

Engage:

What is the primary way you proclaim good news to others, and how is it received?

Reflections:

26

Walking on God's Path

Scripture:

> Many peoples shall come and say,
> "Come, let us go up to the mountain of the LORD,
>   to the house of the God of Jacob;
> that he may teach us his ways
>   and that we may walk in his paths."
> For out of Zion shall go forth instruction,
>   and the word of the LORD from Jerusalem.
> He shall judge between the nations,
>   and shall arbitrate for many peoples;
> they shall beat their swords into plowshares,
>   and their spears into pruning hooks;
> nation shall not lift up sword against nation,
>   neither shall they learn war any more.

—Isaiah 2:3–4

Prayer:

Almighty God, Maker of heaven and earth,

we bow in awe and wonder before your works.
In marvelous orderliness, in stupendous grandeur,
   in soul-stirring beauty you have made your world.
     Where we have marred your beautiful vision,
       forgive us, O Lord.
Where you call upon us to participate with you
   in the fashioning of an unfinished creation,
     grant us wisdom and zeal.
Lord God of hosts, you reign over all the nations,
   give peace in our time.
Help us to obey your call
   to compassion and service toward all.
Help us to find our security and strength,
   not in our own way and will to power,
     but in your way of righteousness and peace,
       Where we have relied on our own strength,
         forgive us, O Lord.
Lord Christ, forgive us indeed,
   for we have sinned against you
     by closing our hearts and our hands
     to the needs of our brothers and sisters.
Help us to carry your cross, and not nail you to it. Amen.

                    —Georgia Harkness, *Grace Abounding*

Hymn:

O Zion, haste, thy mission high fulfilling,
to tell to all the world that God is light,
that he who made all nations is not willing
one soul should perish, lost in shades of night.
Refrain:
Publish glad tidings, tidings of peace;
tidings of Jesus, redemption and release.

Proclaim to every people, tongue, and nation
that God, in whom they live and move, is love;
tell how he stooped to save his lost creation,
and died on earth that we might live above.
(*Refrain*)

—UMH 573:1, 3 (Mary Thomson)

Mary Thomson (1834–1923), the daughter of an Anglican priest, emigrated from England to the United States as a little girl. She lived almost the entirety of her life in Philadelphia where she nurtured a deep love of poetry. Her hymn, "O Zion, Haste," became a favorite in her Episcopal heritage and beyond, keynoting the optimism of the late-nineteenth-century concerning mission.

Engage:

What are the mission projects in which you are involved in your own neighborhood?

Reflections:

27

The Least of These

Scripture:

Then the righteous will answer him, "Lord, when was it that we saw you hungry and gave you food, or thirsty and gave you something to drink? And when was it that we saw you a stranger and welcomed you, or naked and gave you clothing? And when was it that we saw you sick or in prison and visited you?" And the king will answer them, "Truly I tell you, just as you did it to one of the least of these who are members of my family, you did it to me."

—Matthew 25:37–40

Prayer:

God of compassion and mercy,
as I have shared your love with those who suffer,
   you have conducted me and them through life
      to the mansion of peace.
         You call me to serve the least of these—
         my brothers and sisters.
Give me strength to extend help to those in need,

that they may know and love you deeply
and that I may be entitled to your blessing.
You call me to serve the least of these—
my brothers and sisters.
Keep my eyes open to all those in need
whom you have placed in my way.
May I see my blessed Redeemer in each of them
and extend my love to them as you have to me.
You call me to serve the least of these—
my brothers and sisters.
Enable me, by the power of your Holy Spirit,
to rescue those who struggle in life
and offer them a vision of your life-giving love. Amen.

—Dorothy Ripley, *Account*

Hymn:

Rescue the perishing, care for the dying,
snatch them in pity from sin and the grave;
weep o'er the erring one, lift up the fallen,
tell them of Jesus, the mighty to save.
Refrain:
Rescue the perishing, care for the dying;
Jesus is merciful, Jesus will save.

Down in the human heart, crushed by the tempter,
feelings lie buried that grace can restore;
touched by a loving heart, wakened by kindness,
chords that were broken will vibrate once more.
(*Refrain*)

Rescue the perishing, duty demands it;
strength for thy labor the Lord will provide;
back to the narrow way patiently win them;

tell the poor wanderer a Savior has died.
(*Refrain*)

—UMH 591:1, 3–4 (Fanny Crosby)

Engage:

Describe a situation in which you saw Christ "in the least of these."

Reflections:

28

All Creation Praises God

Scripture:

> Holy, holy, holy,
> the Lord God the Almighty,
>   who was and is and is to come.
> You are worthy, our Lord and God,
>   to receive glory and honor and power,
> for you created all things,
>   and by your will they existed and were created.
>
> —Revelation 4:8, 11

Prayer:

We thank you, O God, for the beauty of your world
    that reminds us continuously
        of your goodness and abounding grace.
We thank you, O God, that you have made the world so fair.
    Help us to open our eyes to its beauty,
        and from it to lift our hearts to you.
We thank you, O God, for the ever-changing

beauty of your world,
> for lively lakes and mountains,
> for good friends that make life richer,
> for rest from labor that energizes our work.

We thank you, O God, that in wisdom and love
> you have placed so much beauty in the world
> > for our happiness and blessing.
> Help us to use your good gifts for growth in grace
> > and in service to one another.

We thank you, O God, that you have made the world so beautiful.
> Let our eyes never grow dim to its enchantment
> > nor our souls dull to its lifting power. Amen.

—Georgia Harkness, *Grace Abounding*

Hymn:

Lord of life, beneath the dome
of the universe, thy home,
gather us who seek thy face
to the fold of thy embrace,
for thou art nigh.
Refrain:
Holy, holy, holy, Lord God of Hosts!
Heaven and earth are full of thee!
Heaven and earth are praising thee,
O Lord most high!

While the deepening shadows fall,
heart of love enfolding all,
through the glory and the grace
of the stars that veil thy face,
our hearts ascend.
(*Refrain*)

When forever from our sight
pass the stars, the day, the night,
Lord of angels, on our eyes
let eternal morning rise
and shadows end.
(*Refrain*)

—UMH 687:2–4 (Mary Lathbury)

Mary Lathbury (1841–1913), a multi-talented educator, artist, editor, and poet, gained fame in her own day for her promotion of the Sunday School, Temperance, and Chautauqua movements. This Methodist composed most of her hymns as so-called "laureate of Chautauqua." Her most enduring hymn invites the singer into a dynamic relationship with the Scriptures.

Engage:

What aspects of God's creation draw you into God's love most consistently?

Reflections:

29

Communion of Saints

Scripture:

Therefore, since we are surrounded by so great a cloud of witnesses, let us also lay aside every weight and the sin that clings so closely, and let us run with perseverance the race that is set before us, looking to Jesus the pioneer and perfecter of our faith, who for the sake of the joy that was set before him endured the cross, disregarding its shame, and has taken his seat at the right hand of the throne of God.

—Hebrews 12:1–2

Prayer:

We thank you, O God, for grace abounding
    in the lengthy heritage of faith in the saints of your church.
        You have blessed our lives so richly through them.
    Those who stand in this endless line of splendor
        continue to offer to us the gifts of encouragement and hope.
We thank you, O God, for hallowed memories
    and for the winsome witness of those who lived

so long before us.
Those who stand in this endless line of splendor
    continue to offer to us the gifts of courage and faith.
We thank you, O God, for the faithful of all generations
    who have offered us their spiritual counsel
        and pointed us in the direction of your way and will.
Those who stand in this endless line of splendor
    continue to offer to us the gifts of wisdom and love.
Help us, in the midst of change and turmoil,
    to know that you are strong and loving and secure,
        and will help us move forward in hope and love.
Grant us, we pray, the hope, the courage, and the wisdom
    to carry forward this legacy of love
        in ways that are acceptable to you. Amen.

—Georgia Harkness, *Grace Abounding*

Hymn:

I sing a song of the saints of God,
patient and brave and true,
who toiled and fought and lived and died
for the Lord they loved and knew.
And one was a doctor, and one was a queen,
and one was a shepherdess on the green;
they were all of them saints of God, and I mean,
God helping, to be one too.

They lived not only in ages past;
there are hundreds of thousands still.
The world is bright with the joyous saints
who love to do Jesus' will.
You can meet them in school, on the street, in the store,
in church, by the sea, in the house next door;

they are saints of God, whether rich or poor,
and I mean to be one too.

—UMH 712:1, 3 (Lesbia Scott)

Lesbia Scott (1898–1986) wrote religious dramas for her native
Church of England. Most of her hymns she composed for the use
of her own children. Among these was this selection, written to
commemorate All-Saints Day. Originally published in *Everyday
Hymns for Children* in 1929, it seems to have become more popular in the United States than in Britain.

Engage:

Describe a departed loved one, and what that person still means
to you today.

Reflections:

30

Partners in God's Victory

Scripture:

Then David blessed the LORD in the presence of all the assembly; David said: "Blessed are you, O LORD, the God of our ancestor Israel, forever and ever. Yours, O LORD, are the greatness, the power, the glory, the victory, and the majesty; for all that is in the heavens and on the earth is yours; yours is the kingdom, O LORD, and you are exalted as head above all. Riches and honor come from you, and you rule over all. In your hand are power and might; and it is in your hand to make great and to give strength to all. And now, our God, we give thanks to you and praise your glorious name.

—1 Chronicles 29:10–13

Prayer:

If I know my heart, O glorious Lord,
    it desires no other glory on earth but yours,
        no other wisdom except that which comes from you.
You are the true source of all understanding

which enables me to live in and do your will.
You have given me a deep commitment
  to the end of injustice in this world.
You have filled my soul with a tenderness
  towards all who are degraded and oppressed.
I know that you are pleased with my compassion
  toward all my brothers and sisters
    who are despised by others
    despite your deep love for them.
I remain confident in your promise
  that your kingdom will come
    and replace all hatred, sin, and strife
    with your beloved and peaceable rule.
Therefore, follow with your blessing
  my earnest prayers for the speedy deliverance
    of all those who groan for your redemption.
If you are pleased to use me as a participant
  in your glorious work of peace and justice,
    your will be done here as in heaven! Amen.

                —Dorothy Ripley, *Account*

Hymn:

In the beauty of the lilies
Christ was born across the sea,
with a glory in his bosom
that transfigures you and me;
as he died to make men holy,
let us die to make men free,
while God is marching on.
Refrain:
Glory, glory, hallelujah!
Glory, glory, hallelujah!
Glory, glory, hallelujah!

His truth is marching on.

He is coming like the glory
of the morning on the wave,
he is wisdom to the mighty,
he is honor to the brave;
so the world shall be his footstool,
and the soul of wrong his slave.
Our God is marching on.
(*Refrain*)

—UMH 717:4–5 (Julia Ward Howe)

Julia Ward Howe (1819–1910) was a New York poet of great renown, publishing multiple collections of her verse. In the years leading up to the American Civil War, she became an ardent Unitarian and abolitionist, and a passionate supporter of Abraham Lincoln and the Union. She composed the "Battle Hymn of the Republic" after witnessing a troop review in Washington.

Engage:

Where do you see signs of God's reign of righteousness, justice, and peace in the world?

Reflections:

Original Authors and Sources

Source Abbreviations

EMS   Chilcote, Paul W., ed. *Early Methodist Spirituality: Selected Women's Writings*. Nashville: Kingswood, 2007.

Harkness   Harkness, Georgia. *Grace Abounding: A Devotional Autobiography*. Nashville: Abingdon, 1974.

HOS   Chilcote, Paul W., ed. *Her Own Story: Autobiographical Portraits of Early Methodist Women*. Nashville: Kingswood, 2001.

UMH   *United Methodist Hymnal*. Nashville: United Methodist Publishing House, 1989.

Wesley   Wallace, Charles, Jr., ed. *Susanna Wesley: The Complete Writings*. Oxford: Oxford University Press, 1997.

Numerical Order with Citations

1	Ann Cutler, *Account*	EMS, 229–30
2	Joanna Cook, *Spiritual Experience*	EMS, 215–17
3	Hester Ann Rogers, *Experience*	EMS, 109
4	Mary Entwisle, Manuscript Diary	EMS, 129–30
5	Dorothy Ripley, *Account*	HOS, 135–36
6	Isabella Wilson, *Diary*	EMS, 133
7	Mary Fletcher, *Life*	EMS, 156–57

8	Mary Langston, *Journal*	EMS, 219–20
9	Isabella Wilson, *Diary*	HOS, 62–63
10	Susanna Wesley, *Writings*	Wesley, 227–28
11	Georgia Harkness, *Grace Abounding*	Harkness, 86
12	Hester Ann Rogers, *Experience*	EMS, 227
13	Mrs. Lefevre, *Letters*	EMS, 212
14	Mrs. Lefevre, *Letters*	EMS, 145
15	Isabella Wilson, *Diary*	EMS, 231–32
16	Margaret Davidson, *Life*	EMS, 222–231
17	Hester Ann Rogers, *Experience*	EMS, 113–14
18	Georgia Harkness, *Grace Abounding*	Harkness, 56, 64, 70
19	Georgia Harkness, *Grace Abounding*	Harkness, 128, 142, 145, 158
20	Sarah Ryan, *Account*	EMS, 79–80
21	Mary Tooth, *Account*	EMS, 337
22	Elizabeth Evans, *Adam Bede*	EMS, 235
23	Sarah Crosby, *Account*	EMS, 224–25
24	Susannah Design, Manuscript Journal	EMS, 210–11
25	Dorothy Ripley, *Account*	HOS, 150–51
26	Georgia Harkness, *Grace Abounding*	Harkness, 76, 132, 152
27	Dorothy Ripley, *Account*	HOS, 135
28	Georgia Harkness, *Grace Abounding*	Harkness, 50, 59, 62, 67, 73
29	Georgia Harkness, *Grace Abounding*	Harkness, 22, 44
30	Dorothy Ripley, *Account*	HOS, 135–36

Alphabetical Listing of Authors

Alphabetical Listing of Hymn Writers/Translators

Names	Reading Numbers
Sarah Adams	22
Lydia Baxter	24
Jane Borthwick	23
Mary E. Byrne	17
Elizabeth Clephane	13
Laura Copenhaver	25
Fanny Crosby	2, 12, 14, 15, 16, 27
Frances Havergal	20, 21
Julia Ward Howe	30
Mary Lathbury	28
Jane Marshall	18
Civilla Martin	4
Catherine Noel	6
Christina Rossetti	8, 9
Clara Scott	19
Lesbia Scott	29
Mary Thomson	26
Catherine Winkworth	1, 3, 5, 7, 10, 11

Alphabetical Index of Hymns

Listing of Scripture Texts

Texts (Canonical Order) Reading Numbers

Old Testament (Hebrew Scriptures)

Deuteronomy 6:4–6	1
1 Chronicles 29:10–13	30
Psalm 24:9–10	7
Psalm 46:10–11	23
Psalm 68:7–11	25
Psalm 100:8–9	2
Psalm 113:1–4	5
Psalm 121:1–2, 8	4
Psalm 145:15–18	15
Isaiah 2:3–4	26

New Testament

Matthew 1:20b–21	24
Matthew 5:6–9	17
Matthew 6:8–10	18
Matthew 11:28–30	14
Matthew 25:37–40	27
Luke 2:8–11, 14	8
John 4:13–15	22
John 11:25–27	11

Bibliography

Chilcote, Paul W., ed. *Early Methodist Spirituality: Selected Women's Writings.* Nashville: Kingswood, 2007.

————, ed. *Her Own Story: Autobiographical Portraits of Early Methodist Women.* Nashville: Kingswood, 2001.

Clarke, Adam, ed. *Memoirs of the Late Eminent Mrs. Mary Cooper, of London.* Halifax: William Nicholson, 1910.

Entwisle, Mary. Manuscript Diary. Methodist Archives, John Rylands University Library of Manchester, Manchester, UK.

Harkness, Georgia. *Grace Abounding: A Devotional Autobiography.* Nashville: Abingdon, 1974.

Rogers, Hester Ann. *An Account of the Experience of Hester Ann Rogers.* New York: Hunt & Easton, 1893.

Taft, Zechariah, ed. *Biographical Sketches of the Lives and Public Ministry of Various Holy Women.* Vol. 1. London: Kershaw, 1825.

Wallace, Charles, Jr., ed. *Susanna Wesley: The Complete Writings.* Oxford: Oxford University Press, 1997.

www.ingramcontent.com/pod-product-compliance
Lightning Source LLC
Chambersburg PA
CBHW032231080426
42735CB00008B/812